Contemporary Music of Japan

ÉTUDES TO "5 SCENES"
by Snare Drum solo

Yasuo SUEYOSHI

現代日本の音楽
スネアドラム・ソロによる
"五つの情景"へのエチュード
末吉保雄

1. 威勢よく (con energia) —— 6
2. 少しおどけて (scherzando) —— 8
3. 静かに (calmato) —— 10
4. さあ、行け (marciale) —— 12
5. 帰ろうっと… (rapido) —— 14

Commissioned by
Mizuki AITA

First performance
Mizuki AITA
March 24, 2016
SEIJO Hall
Tokyo, Japan

Recording
CD: Lover on the Staff (Mizuki AITA, *perc.*)
ALCD-116
ALM RECORDS

委嘱
會田瑞樹

初演
會田瑞樹
2016年3月24日
東京・成城ホール

録音
CD: 五線紙上の恋人（會田瑞樹：打楽器）
ALCD-116
ALM RECORDS

スネアドラム・ソロによる "五つの情景" へのエチュード

1. 威勢よく（con erergia） 2. 少しおどけて（scherzando）
3. 静かに（calmato） 4. さあ、行け（marciale） 5. 帰ろうっと…（rapido）

　各曲（楽章）の冒頭に上記のような楽想を表示しました。奏者が、譜を試奏しながら、それぞれに、それぞれの "情景" をイメージし、表現してほしいと願うものです。ただ、多少、作曲者からの "示唆" を注記すれば、
　1：呼び込み（市場か、芝居小屋か）の景気の良さ、いなせな風情。
　2：おかしな唄を歌いながらの行商（飴か、駄菓子か）、その少しばかり、軽薄でいかがわしい趣。
　3：歌舞伎風の舞台の夜。雨だれ、雪、忍びの者。静寂のなかの微細な気配。
　4：出陣の気合い。大門から繰り出す勢い。
　5：打ち出し。ああ面白かった！　帰る足取りも軽く。

　とは言うものの、どうか、楽想表示の先に、日本風に限らない、さまざまなイメージが展開されますように（通奏せずに、いくつか、またはどれかに限っての演奏も自由です）。

　太鼓。作曲者の偏愛する楽器です。そのどれでも、見るだけで音を出したくなります。若いときから日本の伝統音楽に惹かれたのも、多くの民族（俗）音楽を好んだのも、たぶん太鼓のため。とくにそれが、声、笛といっしょになったときの音楽空間は、格別です。

　この曲は、気鋭の打楽器奏者會田瑞樹の、作曲者『個展』（2016年3月）開催にあたり、「スネアのソロ曲を」との求めに応えて作曲されました。會田が学生のとき、旧作のマリンバ・ソロ《ミラージュ》を演奏した縁で、これまでに多くを共演してきました。つまり若い仕事仲間の一人です。ヴィブラフォンのソロ《西へ》（2013）、マリンバとピアノのための《break through》（2015）、トランペットとヴィブラフォンによる《コレスポンダンス XII》（2016）、これらも彼の委嘱を受けて生まれました。

末吉保雄

Études to "5 Scenes" by Snare Drum solo

1. con energia / 2. scherzando / 3. calmato / 4. marciale / 5. rapido

I displayed the theme at the head of each piece (movement) as described above, hoping that players will image and express the "scene" respectively, when trying out with the music sheet. If the composer notes any "suggestions":

1: High-spirited, dashing barkers (at market place or playhouse).

2: Peddlers singing a funny song (selling mom-and-pop candy) , and their looking a little bit frivolous and suspicious.

3: A night scene on the Kabuki-like stage…raindrops, snow, a ninja…with refined signs in silence.

4: The highest spirits of the departure for the front, and the energy in flocking out of the great gate.

5: The close. So interesting it was! Light steps on the way back home.

For all that, I wish a variety of images will be developed through the themes, not bound by Japanese style. (To play not the whole piece but some or one of the selected pieces would be also possible.)

Drums are the instrument that the composer favors intensely. Any sight of them tempts me to make a sound with it. Probably, it was because of this drum's fascination that I have been attracted by Japanese traditional music from my youth, and also fond of a lot of ethnic (folk) music.

This work is commissioned by Mizuki Aita, an energetic percussion player, and composed in respond to his request for a work for snare drum solo, when the composer's *Personal Exhibition* was to be held (March, 2016). Aita performed my old piece "Mirage pour Marimba" in his school days. Because of the relation, we have shared many stages so far. He is, so to speak, one of the young associates that I work with. "To the West" for vibraphone solo(2013), "break through" for marimba and piano （2015）,"Correspondance XII" for trumpet and vibraphone （2016）also came into this world by his commission.

Yasuo Sueyoshi

演奏にあたって

　この作品は末吉保雄先生の傘寿を前に小生が企画し、世田谷区、せたがや文化財団と共同で開催した「末吉保雄作品『個展』〜内に秘めたる声を求めて」において初演されました。末吉先生に、ぜひともスネアドラムのための作品を描いて頂きたく、編成を指定しての作曲委嘱に至りました。

　スネアドラムにはたくさんの音色が「隠されて」います。ヘッドのど真ん中、端を叩き分けるだけで音程は変化します。さまざまなバチによって音色は変化し、時にはハンカチをかぶせたり、肘でヘッドに圧をかけると音程が上下したり、響き線の on と off の時に発生するノイズも音楽になるのではないか…末吉先生とスネアドラムを前にあれこれと試して、先生が永年培われた音風景とスネアドラムが幸せに出会い、このような作品が生まれました。楽章毎に抜粋で演奏することも出来、「独奏」をはじめて試みる演奏者にとってもこんなに素敵なコンサート・エチュードは他に類例がないと思っています。

　第１楽章では「ギロ」のようなバチと通常のバチを使用し「どんと・こい」と歌っているような威勢の良いかけ声が聞こえます。「ギロ・バチ」のゴリゴリとした音色を際立たせてください。

　第２楽章では「ひょっとこの踊り」のようなひょうきんなリズムが、柔らかなバチや紫檀のような重めのバチで軽妙に奏でられます。

　第３楽章は雨だれの音楽。スネアドラムで「静寂」を表現してみてください。雨の日の軒先に立っているだけで、音楽上のヒントを得られるはずです。

　第４楽章では軽快で攻撃的なマーチをリムショットと共に力強く奏でてみてください。

　第５楽章は、和太鼓に用いるような非常に細いバチをスネアドラムで使ってみてください。「追い出しの太鼓」のように、「でてけ、でてけ」のかけ声を口ずさみながら演奏すると、サマになってきませんか？

　たった一台のスネアドラムから豊かな音の世界が導きだされる、魔法のような音楽です。そして随所に、かつて日本の風土の中に響いていたリズムが幻のように浮かび上がるかもしれません。

會田瑞樹

For Playing

　This work was premiered in the "Works of Yasuo Sueyoshi *Personal Exhibition*", which I myself planned for his 80th birthday and was given by Setagaya city and Setagaya Arts Foundation. I would like him to write a work for snare drum solo by all means, and commissioned one with instrumental configurations.

　So many tone colors are "hidden" in the snare drum. Intervals change easily, only by striking the center or the edge of the head. Various drumsticks can make numerous tone colors, and sometimes with the head covered with a handkerchief. Intervals are to go up and down by pressing the head with the elbow, and the noise generated in switching the echo wire on and off could be also making music… After I and Sueyoshi tried out either part of a snare drum, the soundscape he acquired over the years and the snare drum happily had an ideal encounter, which produced this work. I think it so wonderful concert etude with hardly real precedent, even for the performer who challenges a "solo piece" for the first time, as each movement can be extracted.

　In the first movement, hi-spirited barking is heard as if it sings "Go ahead!" by using "guiro"-like sticks and normal drumsticks. Emphasize the scraping sound of "guiro sticks".

　In the second movement, waggish rhythms as in the "Hyottoko" (Japanese clown) dance are played lightly with soft sticks and heavy sticks like sandalwood ones.

　The third movement is music of raindrops. Just express "quietness" on the drum. You have only to stand a while under the eaves on a rainy day to find a musical hint.

　In the fourth movement, just play a springy and sharp march smartly with limb shot.

　In the fifth movement, try such slim sticks on the snare drum as used in Japanese drums. Don't you find your sound in good shape when playing with humming the yells, "Go out! Go out!", as if in 'ejection drums'?

　This is the music which derives so rich a sound world from a single snare drum, like magic. The rhythms once echoed everywhere in Japan might emerge like illusion.

Mizuki Aita

注

音符の五線上の位置は、左端に のように記して区別されている。

E は鼓面の端の方の皮膜を打つ
C は皮膜のほぼ中央上を打つことを意味する

*1 やや太く長い木製の撥。握りのやや上に刻みを入れ、ギロとして用いる

*2 ギロとして用いる時、左の撥を被膜の上、刻み目をやや右（内）に置き、右撥で擦る 矢印上方は奏者前方（外）に、矢印下方は右撥を外から手前に向けて擦る

*3 ギロ撥の一方（楽譜では左方向）を、ドラム被膜上に先端を付け、やや後方を立てて（傾けて）置く

*4 先行音符で皮膜を打ち、そのまま膜状に撥の先端を付けたままにして後続の音符へ

*5 *bis ad lib.* 自由に反復する

*6 スネアドラムスティック（標準的な木製の撥）白抜きの棒と黒太く記しした2種を使い分ける。ここは通常の硬さのもの

*7 竹製のブラシ（ささら）

*8 ワイヤーブラシ（金属製）

*9 スネアドラムスティックの硬めのもの（紫檀など）

*10 撥を被膜上に落とした時の自然なバウンド（弾み）

*11 リムショット（Rim と注記しないときもある）×の記号は第1線または第5線上に記される

*12 四角に括った部分を反復する。×7 は 7 回。tri. は 3 回

*13 con sord. ミュートする。この場合は木綿の布を、被膜上 2/5 ほど覆う

*14 左撥を左腕で皮膜上にしっかりと圧し続け、右撥が打った直後この左の圧力を加減する。
そのピッチが
　ゆるめると ——— 微かに下行し、
　強めると ——— 微かに上行する

*15 senza sord. ミュートを解く。この場合は布を取り外す

*16 撥を被膜上に置きっぱなしにする。ミュートの効果となる。右撥で打つと共振するがこれも効果とする

*17 撥を持たない手の平の指を拡げて、2・3本の指を用いて発音する。×は第1線、第5線以外に記される

*18 senza SN 閉じてあるスネアスプリングを勢いよく少し乱暴に開く。そのノイズを効果とする

*19 左手はテンポを一定に保ち続けるが、右手は加速・加強など可変である。／はフレーズの切れ目。これを記されたパートは無拍子となる。一種のポリテンピ

*20 竹製の細長い箸状の撥

*21 任意に 20 秒、カデンツのようにソロアドリブを挿入できる。但し、この 5 曲で用いられた音型のみを用いる。休符の挿入は自由だが、常に第 5 曲の **Tempo I°** を維持しなければならない

Notes

The Notes on the staff are differentiated as
E: strike near the edge of the drum head.
C: strike near the center of the drum head.

*1   Wooden sticks that are rather long and thick. Notches are cut slightly above the top of the grip to use it as guiro.

*2   When used as guiro, put the left stick on the skin so that notches are placed a bit toward right (inward). Then, rub with the right stick.
Upward arrow means to rub toward the front of the performer and downward arrow means to rub the right stick from outside toward himself.

*3   Place the tip of a side of guiro stick (in the score, to the left direction) on the drum skin and set it with the end inclining at a low angle.

*4   Strike the skin on the preceding note. Leaving the tip of stick on the skin, go on to the following note.

*5   Repeat freely.

*6   Snare drum stick (normal wooden stick). Use two different types, one with outline stick mark and the other with thick black stick mark. Here we use a normal hardness.

*7   Bamboo brush (Sasara)

*8   Wired brush (metallic)

*9 Hard snare drum sticks (such as rosewood)

*10 • • • •••• etc. Natural bound made when the sticks are thrown on the skin.

*11 Rim. Rimshot (sometimes not noted as Rim). × mark is written either on the first line or the 5th line.

*12 Repeat the part within the square. ×7 means repeat 7 times. tri. means three times.

*13 con sord. With mute. In this case, cover 2/5 of the head with a cotton cloth.

*14   Pressure the left stick on the top of the skin with your left arm and as soon as the right stick is struck, control this left pressure.
When that pressure is
lessen —— the pitch goes down slightly.
harden —— the pitch goes up slightly.

*15 senza sord. Without mute. In this case, take off the cloth.

*16 Leave the sticks on the skin. This makes a muting effect. Also when the skin is struck with right stick, it resonates, but this is a muting effect, too.

*17 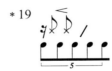 Widen the fingers of palm which you don't hold the stick and use 2 or 3 fingers to hit.
× is written other than 1st and 5th lines.

*18 senza SN Open the snare spring forcefully. The noise is the effect.

*19   The left hand keeps the tempo steadily, but the right hand speed is changeable. / is the end of a phrase. This part has no meter. A kind of polimeter.

*20 Long thin sticks (like chopsticks) made out of bamboo.

*21 You are free to insert solo ad-lib like cadenza for 20 seconds. However, use the note patterns used in these 5 movements. You are free to insert any rests, but keep the tempo of Tempo I of the 5th movement.

*3 ギロ撥の一方をドラム被膜上に先端を付けやや後方を立てて置く　Place the tip of a side of guiro stick on the drum skin and set it with the end inclining at a low angle.
*4 先行音符で皮膜を打ち、そのまま膜状に撥の先端を付けたままにして後続の音符へ　Strike the skin on the preceding note. Leaving the tip of stick on the skin, go on to the following note.
*5 自由に反復　Repeat freely
*6 通常の硬さの撥に持ち替え　Exchange for the SD.stick (wooden, normal)

2

*7 竹製のブラシ（ささら） Exchange for bamboo brush (Sasara)
*8 ワイヤーブラシ（金属製） Wired brush (metallic)

*9 硬めの撥（紫檀など）　Hard snare drum sticks (such as rosewood)

…

3

末吉保雄 作曲
Music by Yasuo SUEYOSHI

*10 撥を被膜上に落とした時の自然なバウンド（弾み）　Natural bound made when the sticks are thrown on the skin.
*11 リムショット（Rimと注記しないときもある）　Rimshot (sometimes not noted as Rim).

© 2016 by Yauo SUEYOSHI　　© 2017 assigned to ONGAKU NO TOMO SHA CORP., Tokyo, Japan.

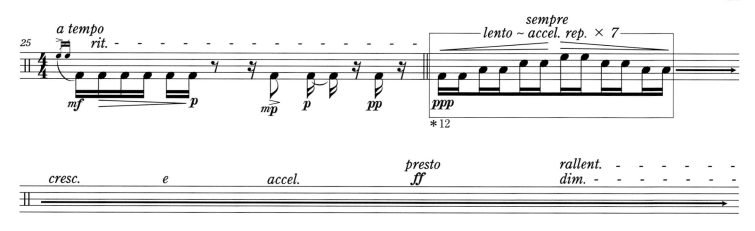

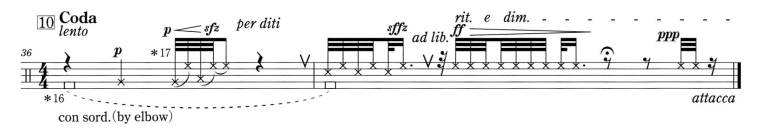

*12 四角に括った部分を反復する。×7は7回。　Repeat the part within the square. ×7 means repeat 7 times.

*13 con sord.　ミュートする。この場合は木綿の布を、被膜上 2/5 ほど覆う　With mute. In this case, cover 2/5 of the head with a cotton cloth.

*14 左撥を左腕で皮膜上にしっかりと圧し続け、右撥が打った直後この左の圧力を加減する。
　　Pressure the left stick on the top of the skin with your left arm and as soon as the right stick is struck, control this left pressure.

*15 senza sord.　ミュートを解く

*16 撥を皮膜上に置きっぱなしにする　Leave the sticks on the skin. This makes a muting effect.

*17 撥を持たない手の平の指を拡げて、2・3本の指を用いて発音する　Widen the fingers of palm which you don't hold the stick and use 2 or 3 fingers to hit.

4

末吉保雄 作曲
Music by Yasuo SUEYOSHI

さあ、行け（marciale）

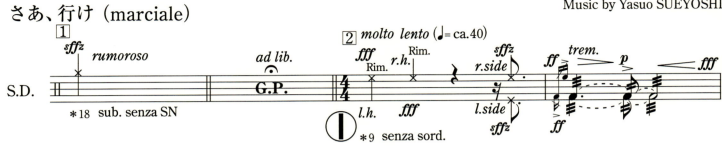

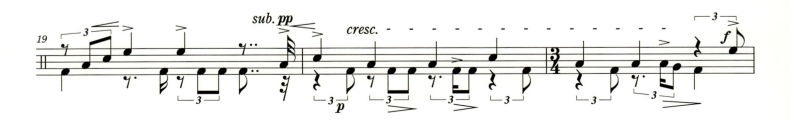

*18　senza SN　スネアスプリングを勢いよく少し乱暴に開く　Open the snare spring forcefully. The noise is the effect

© 2016 by Yauo SUEYOSHI　　© 2017 assigned to ONGAKU NO TOMO SHA CORP., Tokyo, Japan.

5

帰ろうっと…（rapido）

末吉保雄　作曲
Music by Yasuo SUEYOSHI

末吉保雄（すえよし・やすお）
1937年東京生まれ。東京芸術大学、パリ・エコールノルマル音楽院作曲科卒業。1965年フランス国立放送音楽研究所講習生。
作曲活動の当初から声、笛、太鼓のために多くを書き、近年は弦楽器、ピアノつきの歌曲などの分野でも多くを作曲している。
〔主要作品〕
オペラ：《男達》（1967）
　　　　ヴォカリーズのための音楽：No. 1（Sop. 7 Inst. 1959）, No. 2＊（Sop. 2 Fl. 3 Perc. 1965）, No. 3（Sop. Orch. 1968）
歌　曲：《中也の三つの詩》（Sop. Cemb. Fl. Cb. Perc. 1971）,《おかる勘平》＊（北原白秋, Sop. Alt-Fl. Cb. Perc. 1975）
　　　　《君にならびて》（宮澤賢治, Sop. Alt-Fl. 1997）
歌曲集：《或る日の歌より》（Voice Pf. 1999）
室内楽：《伶》（8 Fl. 1970）,《ミラージュ》＊（Mba. 1971）,
　　　　ソロ No.1（8 Tom-tom, 2001）, No. 2（Mba. 2002）, No. 3（Fl. 2003）
　　　　コレスポンダンス I, II（2Cl. 1975, 1976）, Ⅲ, Ⅳ（Fl. Vl. Pf. 1979, 1980）, Ⅴ, Ⅵ（Fl. Perc. 1982, 1984）,
　　　　Ⅶ, Ⅷ（Cb. Perc. 1985）, Ⅸ（2Vl. Vla. Vc. 2000）, Ⅺ（Fl. Cemb. 2003）, Ⅻ（Trp. Mba. 2016）
　　　　《土の歌・風の歌》＊（Pf. for l.h. 2007）,《いっぱいのこどもたち》＊（Pf. for l.h. 2009）
　　　　《西へ》（Vib, 2013）, マリンバとピアノのための《break through》（Mba. Pf. 2015）

Yasuo SUEYOSHI

Born in Tokyo, 1937. Graduated from Tokyo National University of Fine Arts and Music, Ecole Normale de Musique de Paris in composition. From the beginning of composing activities, he wrote many works for voice, flute and drums. In recent years, he has composed many works in the field of string instruments and songs with piano accompaniment.

[Major Works]

Opera:　　　　　"Men" (1967),
　　　　　　　　Music for Vocalise No. 1 (Sop. 7 Inst. 1959), No. 2 *(Sop. 2 Fl. 3 Perc. 1965), No. 3 (Sop. Orch. 1968)

Songs:　　　　　"3 Poems by Chuya" (Sop. Cemb. Fl. Cb. Perc. 1971), "Okaru Kanpei"* (Hakushu, Sop. Alt-Fl. Cb. Perc. 1975),
　　　　　　　　"Kimi ni narabite (With you)" (Kenji, Sop. Alt-Fl. 1997)

Song Album:　　"Aru hi no uta yori (From A Song Sang One Day)" (Voice, Pf. 1999)

Chamber music: "Rei" (8 Fl. 1970), "Mirage"* (Mba. 1971),
　　　　　　　　Solo No.1 (8 Tom-tom, 2001), No. 2 (Mba. 2002), No. 3 (Fl. 2003),
　　　　　　　　Correspondence I, II (2 Cl. 1975, 1976), III, IV (Fl. Vl. Pf. 1979, 1980), V, VI (Fl. Perc. 1982, 1984),
　　　　　　　　VII, VIII (Cb. Perc. 1985), IX (2 Vl. Vla. Vc. 2000), XI (Fl. Cemb. 2003), XII (Trp. Mba. 2016)
　　　　　　　　"Song of the Earth / Voice of the Wind"* (Pf. for l.h. 2007), "plein d' enfants"* (Pf. for l.h. 2009),
　　　　　　　　"To the West" (Vib,2013), "break through" (Mba. Pf. 2015)

＊　音楽之友社刊行／ONGAKU NO TOMO EDTION

皆様へのお願い
　楽譜や歌詞・音楽書などの出版物を権利者に無断で複製（コピー）することは、著作権の侵害（私的利用など特別な場合を除く）にあたり、著作権法により罰せられます。また、出版物からの不法なコピーが行われますと、出版社は正常な出版活動が困難となり、ついには皆様方が必要とされるものも出版できなくなります。
　音楽出版社と日本音楽著作権協会（JASRAC）は、著作者の権利を守り、なおいっそう優れた作品の出版普及に全力をあげて努力してまいります。どうか不法コピーの防止に、皆様方のご協力をお願い申し上げます。

　　　　　　　　　　　　　　　　株式会社 音楽之友社
　　　　　　　　　　　　　　　　一般社団法人 日本音楽著作権協会

LOVE THE ORIGINAL
楽譜のコピーはやめましょう

〈現代日本の音楽〉スネアドラム・ソロによる "五つの情景" へのエチュード

2017年11月10日　第1刷発行

作曲者　末　吉　保　雄
発行者　堀　内　久　美　雄
　　　　東 京 都 新 宿 区 神 楽 坂6の30
発行所　株式会社 音　楽　之　友　社
　　　　電話 03（3235）2111（代）　〒162-8716
　　　　振替 00170-4-196250
　　　　http://www.ongakunotomo.co.jp/

491504

© 2017 by ONGAKU NO TOMO SHA CORP., Tokyo, Japan.

落丁本・乱丁本はお取替いたします。
Printed in Japan.

楽譜浄書：小倉秀一
英訳：壬生千恵子
印刷／製本：錦明印刷（株）

Contemporary Music of Japan

ÉTUDES TO "5 SCENES"
by Snare Drum solo

Yasuo SUEYOSHI

Contemporary Music of Japan

MUSIC FOR VIBRAPHONE AND MARIMBA
(1 player)

Michio MAMIYA

現代日本の音楽

ヴィブラフォンとマリンバのための音楽

間宮芳生

音楽之友社

ONGAKU NO TOMO EDITION